BOUNTY HUNTER

Holly Cefrey

HIGH
interest
books

Children's Press®
A Division of Scholastic Inc.
New York / Toronto / London / Auckland / Sydney
Mexico City / New Delhi / Hong Kong
Danbury, Connecticut

Book Design: Mindy Liu and Michelle Innes
Contributing Editor: Matthew Pitt

Library of Congress Cataloging-in-Publication Data

Cefrey, Holly.
    Bounty hunter / Holly Cefrey.
    p. cm.—(Danger is my business)
    Summary: Introduces the type of work, dangers, and requirements for the
    job of bounty hunter.
    Includes bibliographical references and index.
    ISBN 0-516-24342-X (lib. bdg.)—ISBN 0-516-27865-7 (pbk.)
    1. Bounty hunters—United States—Juvenile literature. 2. Fugitives
from justice—United States—Juvenile literature. [1. Bounty
hunters—Vocational guidance. 2. Vocational guidance.] I. Title. II.
Series.

HV8099.5.C44 2003
363.28'9—dc21
                                                      2003001606

CONTENTS

"I'm not a police officer and I don't work for the government. I'm a hired hand. I am a bounty hunter hot on the trail of a 'skip.' The woman I'm following was arrested and charged with a crime a few months ago. She was freed on bail, on the condition that she appear for her court date. Instead of showing up for her trial, though, she 'skipped' out. Now it's my job to find her, take her to court, and bring her to justice.

"I started my search by contacting her family and friends. They weren't very helpful, but they did give me some recent photos. Next, I studied my skip's paper trail. I researched where she spends her money. The skip's family gave me her most recent receipts. I don't think she has left the city or state. If she has, though, I'm ready to travel anywhere to find her. This job won't end until I have delivered her to the authorities."

A bounty hunter leads a thrilling and sometimes terrifying life. Bounty hunters are expected to capture fugitives. A fugitive is someone who is running away

Like the police officers pictured here, hired bounty hunters have the right to arrest men and women who are running from the law.

from the law. Some fugitives are armed and dangerous. Even worse, they often feel they have nothing to lose.

Bounty hunters may chase skips down dark alleys and streets. They may even break into the skip's house to arrest them. Of course, most skips don't want to be found. Some will even use guns or violence to avoid getting caught. These fugitives are taking advantage of the legal system, and it's up to bounty hunters to stop them.

CHAPTER 1

Hunters for Hire

Bounty hunters track down and capture fugitives. In exchange for this service, they are given a reward. Unlike police officers, bounty hunters are paid for each criminal they arrest and deliver to the authorities.

In the Old West, bounty hunters were called gun-slingers. They chased after people who were dangerous outlaws. Bounty hunters would look for "Wanted" posters of criminals trying to escape justice. Some of the posters would claim that the fugitive being looked for was "Wanted Dead or Alive." This meant that the bounty hunter had permission to hurt, or even kill, his or her target.

Today's bounty hunters are not like those of the past. They aren't likely to track down anyone under the

As the reward offered for Billy the Kid's capture grew, more and more bounty hunters tried to hunt down this fugitive.

conditions of "dead or alive." Even the title "bounty hunter" has been replaced by more current terms. Some of these terms include bail bond enforcers, fugitive recovery agents, and skip tracers.

The James Gang

Jesse James is one of the Old West's most famous figures. He led a group called the James Gang. The gang would boldly rob banks, trains, and stagecoaches in broad daylight. They killed many people while trying to steal money. The gang roamed the United States for over fifteen years. No matter how hard the authorities tried to catch James, he always seemed to stay a step ahead. Finally, Tom Crittenden, the governor of Missouri, decided to offer a bounty. He offered a $10,000 reward for the capture—or death—of James. A member of the James Gang named Robert Ford took the governor up on his offer. In 1882, he shot and killed Jesse James. When Ford tried to collect the reward, though, he was charged with murder.

Jesse James escaped the law on so many occasions, authorities decided to offer a bounty. This bounty would be given in exchange for the capture of James—dead or alive.

By charging steep bail amounts, courts know that the defendants will have to rely on bond agents if they want their temporary freedom.

The Business of Bounty

When people are charged with crimes of which they claim to be innocent, they are arraigned, or brought to a court of law. At the arraignment, the accused person appears before a judge. The judge decides if the defendant, or accused person, can post bail. Bail is money that the defendant pays the court. In exchange for this payment, the court releases the defendant from police custody. However, accused people released on bail are not entirely free. They still have to appear at their trial. The trial will determine if the person is innocent or guilty of the crime. Bail money is returned to defendants once they appear at their trial date.

Special Agents

Bail bond agencies loan money to defendants to pay their bail. These defendants usually pay about 10 percent of the bail, in cash, to the agency. Defendants must also prove that they own items equal in worth to their total bail amount. These items, called collateral, include homes and automobiles.

Before loaning defendants the money, bail bond agents run a background check. They check the defendant's personal character and financial records. They try to guess whether the accused person will appear for a court date, or try to skip it. Agents post and sign a bail bond with the court clerk. This written contract allows defendants to go free until the day of their trial.

The bail bond agent pictured here is scheduled to meet with a new client. The client is accused of a crime and must post bail before being released.

Skip Protection

What if the accused fails to show up for his or her trial? That's when a bounty hunter may be called in.

Once a defendant skips his or her court date, that person becomes a fugitive. Defendants may skip their court appearances for several reasons. Some defendants don't want to be separated from their friends and family. Some may be planning on committing more crimes. Others do it because they think that they can get away with it.

It's the job of a bounty hunter to see that a fugitive doesn't escape the law. Bounty hunting is the business of catching fugitives. A bounty hunter's role is important to the criminal justice system. Bounty hunters are the last line of defense in bringing fugitives to their trials.

DID YOU KNOW

More than 30 percent of bail bond agents are women.

CHAPTER 2

Running From the Law

Each time a fugitive flees justice, bail bond agents get nervous. After all, they've loaned a lot of money to the accused criminal. They expected the defendant to keep his or her promise. If the fugitive escapes for good, the courts keep the bail bond agent's money.

This is why bounty hunters are hired. If bounty hunters can track down fugitives, bail bond agents won't lose their money to the courts. Of course, bail bond agents have to pay successful bounty hunters for their services. However, it's worth it to them to give up some of their money, rather than lose it all.

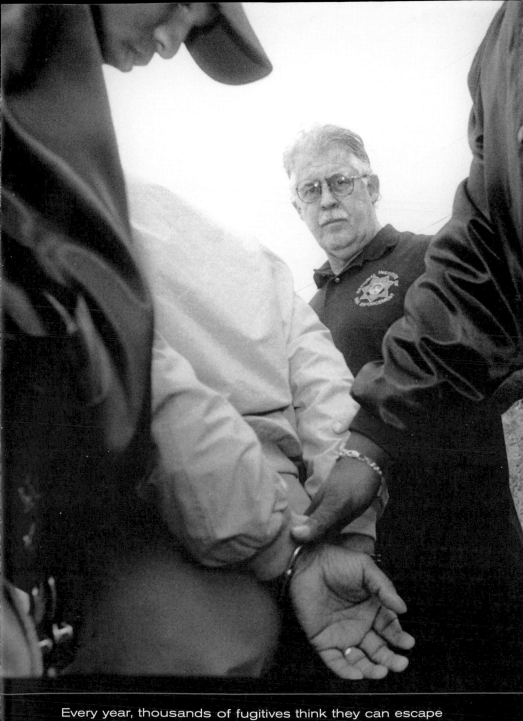

Every year, thousands of fugitives think they can escape justice. Again and again, bounty hunters set out to prove those fugitives wrong.

Tools of the Trade

Bail bond agents have the legal right to arrest skips. Once bail bond agents hire a bounty hunter, that hunter also has the power to arrest the skip.

Of course, this doesn't mean that the skip will always *respect* that power. When making arrests, bounty hunters rely on weapons and tools to keep them safe. They wear body armor and bulletproof vests. They often carry handguns, shotguns, stun guns, or batons. When they're about to arrest someone, they usually keep pairs of handcuffs handy.

However, most bounty hunters rely on a far better tool: their minds. Bounty hunters are tracking down people who don't want to be caught. Instincts, acting skills, and disguises go a long way in helping bounty hunters with their searches. Most of a bounty hunter's job involves doing research. They need to speak with the skip's friends, family members, and co-workers. They need to figure out what that fugitive is thinking. They must find out the skip's patterns of movement. Where are they hiding? What might their next move be? In other words, bounty hunters trap more skips with their wits than their muscle.

How Big Is the Bounty?

Bounty hunters typically receive 10 percent of the bail amount for their services. If a fugitive's bail is $25,000, a bounty hunter might charge a fee of $2,500. Bounty hunters also collect other expenses. For instance, sometimes bounty hunters have to track skips across the country. If that happens, they can charge the bail bond agency with their food, hotel, and car rental costs. If the fugitive flees to another state, bounty hunters may charge 20 percent of the bail amount. Their rate also depends on how much time they've been given to catch their skips. If the

When setting a bail amount, judges often consider whether the accused is a flight risk. In other words, how likely is it that the defendant will become a fugitive?

bounty hunter only has days to catch a skip, that hunter may charge up to 50 percent of the bail amount!

Tricks of the Trade

Bounty hunters begin most searches at police stations. A city or town's police force is often overworked. Any case solved by a professional bounty hunter means one less fugitive the police need to worry about. Sometimes, the police are glad to help the hunter out.

After going to the police, bounty hunters speak with a skip's friends and family. These people will often be more clearheaded than the skip. They don't want to see their friend get into more trouble. They certainly don't want to see their friend harmed while running from the law. Therefore, they may be willing to provide hints about where the skip is hiding. If friends and family members do give clues, bounty hunters must take careful notes. Any piece of information could be the one that solves the puzzle. Of course, bounty hunters also have to watch their backs. Suppose the bounty hunter is interviewing the skip's roommate. Just at that moment, the skip stops by the apartment to pick up some clothes. If the skip is carrying a weapon and the bounty hunter is unarmed, a deadly situation might arise.

Some bounty hunters own or rent vans and trucks and pretend to be repairpersons. This gives them an excuse to park near the fugitive's home and snoop on the skip.

Sneak Attacks

What if the skip's family and friends aren't being helpful? What if the bounty hunter has very little information to go on? That's where their craftiness comes into play. Bounty hunters have come up with some clever ways to track down their targets.

For instance, bounty hunters may have their skip's phone number, but not his or her address. They might call that number and chat with the skip. They'll pretend to belong to a company that wants to give the skip a cash prize. They'll claim that all they need to know is the skip's address. As soon as they have that, they say, they can send the prize. More often than not, the skip will quickly and eagerly give out that address. Little does the fugitive know that the so-called prize is an arrest warrant!

Some bounty hunters use disguises to arrest their skips, too. For instance, they might have themselves wrapped inside a giant box. Then a friend, posing as a delivery person, will wheel them to the skip's front door. When the skip signs for the box, the bounty hunter pops out and makes the arrest.

Reasonable Force

Each state has strict laws about how bounty hunters can, and cannot, operate. Bounty hunters must obey these laws to the letter. Otherwise, they could be the ones paying bail and standing trial!

To get a skip into custody, bounty hunters sometimes must use force. This can lead to tense moments.
Bounty hunters have to expect anyone running from
the law to be armed and dangerous. However, they
also must use caution when arresting skips. They may
use force if the skip resists arrest, but it must be reasonable force. If bounty hunters kill or seriously injure
fugitives who have surrendered, they may be sued.
They may even go to jail for their actions.

DID YOU KNOW

At any given time, the Federal Bureau of
Investigation (FBI) is looking for more than
twelve thousand fugitives.

CHAPTER 3

Hot on the Trail

What would it feel like to be a bounty hunter tracking down a skip? What kind of dangers would you come across?

This chapter follows a fictional character named Harriet Mackenzie. Harriet has been bounty hunting for twenty years. She's just been hired for a big case. In the pages ahead, Harriet describes her chase, every step of the way.

Harriet Tells Her Tale

"You never know how tricky catching your next skip will be. One skip simply held out his hands to be cuffed when he saw me approaching. He realized that

Experienced bounty hunters know they can never get too confident when tracking down a skip. Their targets often act recklessly, which makes them dangerous.

by skipping his trial, he was making things harder on himself. Other skips flee across the country. Once I catch them, though, I make them return a lot sooner than they had planned. I carry a pistol but have never needed to use it. That's not to say my career hasn't brought danger. It's a good thing I have taken jujitsu lessons for half of my life.

"Some skips are petty thieves. They might have a stack of unpaid parking tickets. Others are hardened criminals. The important thing is that each skip is running from the law. Skips decide that they don't want to be judged for what they've done. Someone willing to run from the law is a desperate person. They may commit another crime, or harm anyone that gets in their way. It's my job to keep these desperate fugitives from hurting other people.

"The skip I'm following now, Carrie, is a career criminal. She picks people's pockets and runs away with whatever she grabs. A few months ago, however, she was charged with a far more violent crime— robbing a business at gunpoint. The bail bond agency

Though arresting skips rarely leads to violence, bounty hunters must train and keep themselves in tip-top condition. They don't want to meet a skip who can outmuscle them.

that hired me wants her brought in within a month. Carrie's a slippery skip, so it's going to be tough to beat the clock."

Beginning to Trace

"I start by making a list of all the cities Carrie has lived in, and the jobs she's held. Her full name is Carrie Shroeder, but it turns out she's gone by different names. Some of her aliases include Carrie Schneider and Cathy Shaffer.

"The next thing I do is call her brother, Greg. He is anxious when I tell him his sister is a fugitive. It turns out that he helped pay his sister's bail. He promised his house as collateral to the bond agency. In exchange, the agency paid his sister's bail. Carrie wasn't too grateful, it seems! If she isn't found, the agency will sell Greg's house in order to pay the court."

Neighborhood Watch

"Greg promises to call me if his sister stops by. I've gotten similar promises from Carrie's parents and her last employer.

OWN & XEDO RENTALS & SALES

BAIL BONDS

$ BUY/SELL $ GOLD $ COINS JEWELRY SILVER

In the United States, bail bond agents have had the right to arrest defendants who skip their trials since 1873.

"My next move is to visit Carrie's apartment. Of course, I don't expect her to open the door and let me in. In fact, I'll bet she's no longer staying there. My goal is to visit Carrie's neighbors. They're pretty frightened when I tell them Carrie's a fugitive. Her next-door neighbor, Kyle, thinks he knows where she might be. Last week, Kyle overheard Carrie on her cell phone. She was talking to a guy named Chad.

FBI TEN MOST WANTED FUGITIVE

Aliases: Jack Avery, Mike L. Buchanan, Allan Waagner, Mike L. Bochanan, Roger Allan Clay, Roger Allan Waagner, Clayton A. Waagner, Rober A. Waagner, Rodger Allen Waagner, Roger A. Waagner, Roger Allen Waagner, Robert Allen Waagner, Roger Alan Waagner, Roger Wagner, Steve Bruenberg, Randy Miller, Jack Fisher, Kenny Logan, David Gillies, John Logan, William Small, Steve Grumby, Charles Moore, Steve Bruenbard, Robert Payne, Robert Mills, Eric Oswald, David Long, Rick Mullins, Ronald Johnson, Robert Sales, John Roner, Randy Taylor, Steve Vetter, Steve Gruenberg, John M. Baker, John Michael Baker, Roy Mason, Bryan Butler, Brad Outlaw, Ryan Murphey, Anthony Lowe, Scott Wesley McKenzie, Scott W. McKenzie, Leon Maifield, Tim Stephens, Colin Joseph Vincent, Colin J. Vincent, Jeff Lear, Darren L. Barthel, Rex H. Turner, Jon M. Baker, Jon Michael Baker

DESCRIPTION

Date of Birth:	August 25, 1956		
Place of Birth:	North Dakota		
Height:	6'1"	**Hair:**	
Weight:	175 to 220 pounds	**Eyes:**	Brown/Gray
Build:	Medium	**Complexion:**	Green
Occupation:	Unknown	**Sex:**	Light
Scars and Marks:		**Race:**	Male
Remarks:		**Nationality:**	White
			American

_____ has scars on his right knee, right ankle, and nose. Due to previous frostbite injuries on his hand and toes, have limited use of his left hand and may walk with a limp. He is known to be pro-life and has, in the past, allegedly made threats against abortion clinics and doctors. He has survivalist skills and may be heavily armed.

CAUTION

_____ IS BEING SOUGHT FOR ESCAPING FROM FEDERAL CUSTODY IN ILLINOIS, BANK ROBBERY IN PENNSYLVANIA, FEDERAL FIREARMS VIOLATIONS IN TENNESSEE, AND CARJACKING IN MISSISSIPPI. ALL OF THESE CRIMES OCCURRED IN 2001.

CONSIDERED ARMED AND EXTREMELY DANGEROUS

IF YOU HAVE ANY INFORMATION CONCERNING THIS PERSON, PLEASE CONTACT YOUR <u>LOCAL FBI OFFICE</u> OR THE NEAREST <u>U.S. EMBASSY OR CONSULATE</u>.

REWARD

The FBI is offering a reward of up to $50,000 for information leading directly to the arrest of

The FBI works hard to let the public know when a fugitive has crossed state lines. Doing this helps bounty hunters recover their skips.

He remembered Carrie saying, 'Chad, if you're sure the restaurant has no alarm system, I'll help you out. Just send me the airline tickets.' Two days after the phone call, Carrie was gone."

"I dig through a trash can in the hallway of Carrie's apartment building. Sure enough, there's an envelope inside addressed to C. Shroeder. The return address is from Louisiana. Best of all, there's a note inside, signed 'Chad.' Chad even named the airline Carrie flew on her trip."

Because Carrie crossed state lines, the FBI issued an unlawful flight to avoid prosecution (UFAP) warrant for her arrest. Posters of her face will be hung in post offices across the country.

Quickly, Harriet buys a ticket to New Orleans. She spends her flight researching Louisiana bounty law. Once she lands and checks in to her hotel, Harriet goes to work. She begins showing photos of Carrie in local stores. She hopes this work pans out. Harriet's time is ticking down. If Harriet doesn't catch her skip soon, she won't get paid. Her reputation as a bounty hunter might suffer. Worst of all, Carrie will be free to commit more crimes.

Money Talks

Like many bounty hunters, Harriet often rewards people who provide her with clues about a skip. If the bounty hunter's fee is $2,000, it's worth it to part with $100 for good information. Especially since that information helps the bounty hunter wrap up one case, and begin the next one, much sooner.

"I approach Chad's next-door neighbor with $50. I tell him I'm looking for information on a fugitive named Carrie Shroeder. He tells me he doesn't know anyone by that name. Remembering that the envelope from Chad was addressed to 'C. Shroeder,' I try again. 'What about Cathy Shroeder?' This name rings a bell. Just to be sure, I ask the neighbor to describe Cathy. He says she was about 5'6" tall, with blonde hair and green eyes. This sounds like my skip. I show him a picture of her and he nods. He tells me he's seen this woman with Chad. Now I know that Carrie's using one of her aliases.

"Chad's neighbor overheard Chad telling Carrie he'd meet her at a restaurant tonight called The Roundup.

From this tip, I drive to the restaurant and meet the owner. He remembers Carrie from the photo, too. He says he's seen her at the restaurant each night for a week, with a male friend. Once the restaurant owner learns that Carrie's a career criminal, he gets concerned. He's even more concerned when I tell him that I think Carrie and Chad are planning on robbing his restaurant."

Smoking Out the Skip

It's time for Harriet to go on a stakeout. She rents a van. Then she has a sign made that reads, "Plumbing Solutions, Inc." She sticks this sign to the side of her van. Harriet parks her vehicle by the restaurant's front door.

"At 6:30 P.M., I see Carrie and Chad pull up to the restaurant. Carrie is putting something in her jacket. Its gleam reflects off a street lamp. It's a gun. However, she places the jacket in the car and walks into the restaurant without it. Next, I call the owner. I tell him I'm watching from the van. If Carrie or Chad say anything suspicious about the van, the owner needs to pretend he's having a problem with his kitchen sink. Moments later, I phone the local sheriff. I ask for his help in making the arrest. He tells me he'll send two squad cars with four police officers as backup.

"Two hours later, Chad and Carrie exit the restaurant. The second they do, I rush out of the van. 'Carrie,' I yell, 'you're under arrest for unlawful flight to avoid prosecution.' Both Chad and Carrie are shocked. I've caught them off-guard. However, the next few moments are tense and terrifying. I know Carrie's gun is in the car. I don't know, though, if Chad is concealing a deadly weapon beneath his jacket.

"I never find out the answer. Like most criminals, Chad is more worried about himself than his friend. He sprints away. I let him go—he's not my target. Carrie sees my pistol, and the sheriff's squad car. She places her hands on the hood of my van and surrenders. I can make the arrest, and my heart can stop racing!"

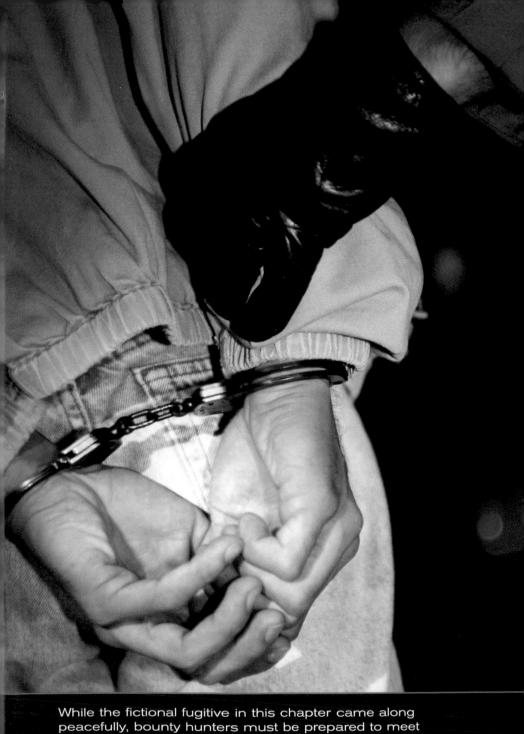

While the fictional fugitive in this chapter came along peacefully, bounty hunters must be prepared to meet any resistance.

CHAPTER 4

Career Hunting

A Growing Need

Recently, the size of many police forces around the United States has been reduced. This may be due to cuts in local budgets and spending. Some no longer have enough officers to seek out skips. Bounty hunters help relieve police officers' overwhelming workload.

At the same time, prisons are more overcrowded than ever. The cost of feeding, housing, and guarding defendants who are waiting for their trials keeps rising. More judges are releasing minor offenders on bail. This keeps the prisons less crowded. Of course, it also keeps bounty hunters busy.

As overcrowding in prisons grows worse and worse, bounty hunters may find a greater demand for their services.

DID YOU KNOW

Three states—Illinois, Oregon, and Kentucky—outlaw bounty hunting.

Starting Out

Bail bond agencies look for bounty hunters who make smooth and peaceful arrests. These bounty hunters are more likely to use their heads and voices—rather than their fists and weapons—to catch a skip. Bounty hunters who use too much force may wind up in trouble. They could be sued, and so could the agency that hired them.

New bounty hunters can also make a splash by catching skips that have eluded other hunters. They can ask a bond agency to let them take a crack at solving the agency's unfinished cases. They are proving their skills to the agency. If they're successful, the grateful agency will give them more work.

If bounty hunters fail to follow the laws of the land, or to use reasonable force, the results can be deadly and tragic. This man was killed in an encounter with a bounty hunter.

The Seekers sometimes employ a weapon, called a taser (seen above), to stun aggressive skips.

Money Matters

Bounty hunters can make a good amount of money in their field. However, they have to be prepared for low-income months. Many bail amounts are fairly low, around $5,000. In this case, a bounty hunter may only make $500. Other months can bring in a $20,000 paycheck for catching one fugitive. Bounty hunters have to take each job seriously, no matter what it pays. Otherwise, they won't get future hires.

Seeking New Solutions

Joshua Armstrong is the leader of a highly trained, seven-person team of bounty hunters called the Seekers. The Seekers want to do more than just catch skips. They want to set them on the right path. The first step is for the fugitive to face his or her trial.

The Seekers are based in New Jersey. Each member uses a code name while working. This way, no criminal can track down the Seekers or their loved ones. Seekers stay in great shape. They are required to lift weights, run, box, and practice martial arts several times a week. They also carry 9-mm semi-automatic handguns. Sometimes, they use scopes that can trace a person's body heat through a wall. They also use air tasers to shock skips with electric charges.

However, the Seekers use stealth more than strength. They dress in black jackets and wear black masks. They try to catch fugitives off-guard. Often, they pick the lock of a skip's apartment or house before dawn. They might pull the sheets off the

The Seekers try to do more than simply capture skips. They try to convince skips that by trying to escape the law, they're heading down the wrong path.

surprised skip's bed and explain that it's time to go. If the skip asks who sent the Seekers, Armstrong answers, "You did."

Armstrong's methods are definitely working. The Seekers' capture rate is a whopping 85 percent! The average rate of catching skips is only 50 percent. All seven Seekers rarely work on the same case together.

They do work in pairs or trios, though. The members constantly gather and share information with one another. They insist on treating skips with respect. They want to avoid violence. For example, their shotguns are filled with rubber bullets. While these rubber bullets hurt, they don't pierce the skin.

The Seekers believe that skips can reform and become better citizens. Armstrong points out that the Seekers arrest most skips on Mother's Day, Christmas, and Thanksgiving. Even while running from justice, most skips still care about their families. Once the skips visit their parents, the Seekers arrest them.

Many fugitives' families know that the Seekers aim to arrest skips peacefully. Because of this, the families are more willing to give the Seekers information. The Seekers believe that people will respond best when treated with respect. After all, a bounty hunter's job is to capture skips, not judge them. Joshua Armstrong's group might be leading bounty hunters in a bold new direction. He also might be making the streets a bit safer for everyone.

alias (**ay**-lee-uhss) a false name, especially one used by a criminal

arraigned (uh-**raynd**) to be called before a court

bail (**bayl**) the sum of money paid to a court to allow someone accused of a crime to be set free until his or her trial

bounty (**boun**-tee) a reward offered for the capture of a criminal

cartridge (**kar**-trij) a container that holds bullets and the explosive that fires them

collateral (kuh-**lat**-ur-uhl) a person's property that is equal in value to a loan of money he or she has been given

custody (**kuhss**-tuh-dee) when a person is arrested by the police

defendant (di-**fen**-duhnt) the person in a court case who has been accused of a crime or who is being sued

eluded (i-**lude**-ed) to have escaped from someone

fugitive (**fyoo**-juh-tiv) someone who is running away, especially from the police instincts (**in**-stingkts) behavior that is natural rather than learned

jujitsu (joo-**jeet**-soo) a Japanese form of martial arts

prosecution (**pross**-uh-kyoo-shun) a legal action in a court of law against a person accused of a crime

reasonable (**ree**-zuhn-uh-buhl) fair or sensible

recovery (ri-**kuhv**-ur-ee) getting or bringing something or someone back

reputation (rep-yuh-**tay**-shun) a person's worth or character, as judged by other people

skip (**skip**) to leave a place quickly or secretively; a person who has not appeared in court to be tried for a crime

stakeout (**stayk**-out) to watch a place for the appearance of a person or persons

stealth (**stelth**) to be secret and quiet

warrant (**wor**-uhnt) an official piece of paper that gives permission to do something, such as arrest a person

Donkin, Andrew. *Crime Busters*. New York: DK Publishing, Inc., 2001.

January, Brendan. *FBI*. New York: Scholastic Library Publishing, 2001.

Owen, David. *Police Lab: How Forensic Science Tracks Down and Convicts Criminals*. Westport, CT: Firefly Books LTD, 2002.

Wiese, Jim. *Detective Science: 40 Crime-Solving, Case-Breaking, Crook-Catching Activities for Kids*. Hoboken, NJ: Wiley, John & Sons, Inc., 1996.

Winters, Paul A. *Crime*. San Diego, CA: Greenhaven Press, 1997.

Organizations

American Bail Coalition
1725 Desales Street, N.W., Suite 800
Washington, DC 20036
Telephone: (202) 659-6547 or (800) 375-8390
Fax: (202) 296-8702
www.americanbailcoalition.com

National Institute of Bail Enforcement
PMB 268–3105 North Ashland Avenue
Chicago, IL 60657
Telephone: (815) 675-0260
Fax: (815) 675-9716
www.bounty-hunter.net

Web Sites

America's Most Wanted

www.amwweb.com

This is the official Web site for the popular TV show of the same name. The show has used tips and information from its viewers to capture over seven hundred criminals!

FBI's Most Wanted

www.fbi.gov/mostwant/topten/fugitives/fugitives.htm

This frequently updated site gives pictures and descriptions of today's most dangerous fugitives. Find out who the bounty hunters are trying to track down!

First Gov for Kids—Fighting Crime

www.kids.gov/k_crime.htm

This site gives you information on different kinds of crimes. It also provides links on how to prevent crime in your neighborhood.

INDEX

A
agency, 11, 24, 26, 36
aliases, 26, 30
arraigned, 10
arrest, 5–6, 16, 20–21, 41

B
bail, 4, 10–11, 20, 26, 34, 38
bounty hunter, 4–7, 12–14,
    16, 18–22, 29–30, 34, 36,
    38–39, 41

C
collateral, 11, 26
crime, 4, 11, 24
criminal, 6, 14, 24, 31, 39

D
defendant, 10–12, 14

F
FBI, 29
force, 21, 36
fugitive, 4–6, 12–14, 16, 18, 20,
    26–27, 30, 38–39

G
gunslingers, 6

H
handcuffs, 16

J
judge, 10

L
loan, 11

About the Author

Holly Cefrey is a freelance writer and researcher. She is a member of the Authors Guild and the Society of Children's Book Writers and Illustrators.